Blue Exodus

Blue Exodus

Hussain Ahmed

ISBN: 978-1-949039-45-0

Orison Books
PO Box 8385
Asheville, NC 28814
www.orisonbooks.com

Distributed to the trade by Itasca Books
1-800-901-3480 / orders@itascabooks.com
www.itascabooks.com

Cover photos courtesy of Shutterstock.

Manufactured in the U.S.A.

ORISON
BOOKS

CONTENTS

I

II

III

Time is kept in a box that does not remember dates.

−Kwame Dawes

I

BLUE

The Mediterranean remains blue across centuries of swallowing.
Because it is not a cemetery, it does not date its memories.

On the sky is a diary that catalogued the bodies lost to the sea.

In the language of a gong, water clashed against the rocks,
an elegy to the fish that embalmed our dead inside their cold bodies.

After the new millennium, I learned to forget what I cannot save.

A seed vault was built outside a deserted city—obscured with grief,
I searched for familiar faces from the shadows on the walls.

Now, every song in a foreign tongue sounds like a prayer.

COSMOLOGY OF THE CLOUD WITH BABA AS THE RAIN MAKER

I

The sky was a rolag, carded with grief and dew.
We were made in the image of our dead

because God relied on recycling
to keep the earth going around the sun.

II

Each of my father's eyes was a globe of brown worms,
or a bulb of sperm cells swimming towards an egg in search of light.

He no longer reads the Qur'an without his glasses.
The ritual of whirling in the first rain has no origin story.

III

Today, the sky looked freshly molded from clay,
I jumped into the rain with my hands raised to the sky.

No one stays in it for long, so it doesn't unmake the scars
on our heads—healing and almost forgotten.

IV

The puddle sometimes gets large, it drags a child away.

Everyone lost to the water was recovered without their eyes,
that's how I know a fish loves to swallow whatever resembles a lamp.

PRAYER

I held a snowball in my hand
when I heard the muezzin's call.

Halfway in prayer, I doubted
if this God could distinguish brown eyes.

I worried less, and sought intercession
with the tongue I sinned with.

For the first time,
I prayed in a new country—

with the tongue I inherited
from a dead man.

WI-FI IN A FLOATING COLONY

Baba's prayer rugs are maps of floating colonies,
or ram furs, sacrificed the day we got our names.

Fine-sand sipped through the fingers of a palmist,
he faced the rising sun and said a prayer for everyone lost to the flood.

In silence, we watched our parents,
until we became fluent in the language of grief.

A new country emerged from the shores after the flood,
and survivors were mistaken for tourists because they were half-naked.

Sacrifices were made after each prayer,
until there was no rooster to usher the rise of the sun.

Feathers are enough to make any country float in the wind,
and like a broken magazine, each scar is a radio frequency for rescue.

Descendants of this floating colony are now cave builders.
On the walls, they've left signs for how to keep lamps burning inside an ebb.

Because we cannot rely on the sky to shine a light on us,
we held hands in prayer and called the circle a planet.

COSMOLOGY OF MY ROOM AS A PLANET OF ROSARIES

Each click of the beads revives old qasida I don't know how to chorus
because the composers left no diary, or they left it drenched in ink.

The rising of my chest is music, inherited from what could kill me.
This room has the memory of Baba's childhood and now it has mine.

I hope it won't mistake them for my grandfather's, or his sibling's.
Rosaries were the first signs I could point at for God's many names.

In a diary of ninety-nine chapters, every page was made of a dead daisy
because they were shaped like discs that safeguard memories buried in them.

I was born with names for everything that fit inside my mouth, but
I failed so many times at naming each prayer bead after blurred planets.

Beneath this bed of lilies is a well with a rope-swing for khalwa.
I tell different stories about this room, it seems the size of Jupiter to me

but it is barely Pluto to the men who lived in it for decades. This house
grew smaller with each birthday, but the rosaries still fit around my neck.

LINEAGE

I

Every lineage has a river.

I come from two bahar,
neither is of honey nor milk.

Bahar is what kept
our hearts drumming

as we walked out from
a makabarta, wherein

bloomed mustards
are now tucked away

from the glance of the sun.

II

On this beach, I imagined
Officer S was back

from a peace-keeping mission
without his index finger.

Unwilling to unclothe his grief,
I asked about his wedding ring

Instead. He took off his helmet
and kissed his head to the ground.

III

I stared at the browning horizon
and praised the walls, where names
of missing soldiers were etched.

The river flows through seasons of loss,
and bahar is how I measured the distance
between grieving hearts.

PARALYSIS

Meknes

Tongues bulged
with prayers

in a city about to melt
in the heat wave.

At the end of a juma'at prayer,
the wards were packed

with patients who lost
control of their nerves.

For two months,
the congregation gathered

facing the east with palms
cupped to the sky.

Butterflies nestled in their hands
and in November

a garden of sunflowers withered.
Their chloroplasts were clogged

with jet engine oil.
Pilgrims arrived Meknes

to celebrate Moulid, with tongues
lubricated in contaminated olive.

The sea reflected the sky—
a spinneret for shadows.

Plankton floated on the saltwater,
unable to swim against the current.

PARADISE

I

In this paradise, a baobab died
with roots inside the ground.

Superstition becomes an experiment
when there's faith to outlive a drought.

The soldier's bag was packed with bitter-kolas,
because they cure a thousand ailments or more.

If you own what could be inherited,
then death becomes a cure,

and without history, even God is mortal.

II

Paradise is where the windows are always closed.
There is a tray at every entrance to its library,

heaped with the ashes from the incense we light up
anytime we say prayers for the soldiers who feasted with us

before they left for the frontlines.

III

Paradise is where the petals of nameless
flowers deflate the grief in the air.

It is forbidden to say this aloud: our prayers were
unanswered; the soldiers did not return—alive.

BRIDGE

I

On a bridge,
poled with the bones of men

who were once scared
of the cold water,

a soldier stood in the center,
his khaki soaked in blood.

II

I was made to love sargassum
for how well it floats on the sea,

as a lifeline for voyagers
who could see silhouettes

of their past lives
strutting on the water.

III

A soldier who swallowed his whistle
must find a way home from the wild.

Suppose I am on the bridge with the soldier,
and we count the stars

from the reflections below.
Suppose every man in a khaki

needs no whistle to be found
or never gets lost for daring to leave home.

IV

In the wake of his passing,
I made decorations of the scars I could not hide,

and a shrine of where he last prayed
in his favorite purple shirt.

ORIGIN OF MOURNING

It all began like a love story,   snow perched on flowers   swaying so well
you would know   they have become rare for all the anthers that got blown away.
The origin of mourning ends where it all began—   a deer's heart   was
wrapped in a foil.   I have managed to close my eyes to retain this weight,   but I see a
candle burning its wick slowly, on a restaurant table. Outside, a bird hits its beak on the glass
window,   the bird sees itself and will not let its reflection remain—unsure, it might not
make it back home if half itself   remains where no one ever looks for anything with wings.

The flames grow taller and now I see a face, like a bulb of garlic pulled from the ground
soaked in blood.   Love does not make me see any better, it blinds me from telling apart
dimples and scars.   The world grows fatter on missing memories, I still have the keys
to the room   where I stored the aerial photographs   of our old house.

I crave warmth when it gets dark,   except for the candles in the restaurant. The origin of mourning is the burning that does not eat up my eyes. It began when our shadows were the only map we had.   It grew taller, sometimes it followed behind and then shoulder to shoulder we matched   with sore gaits. The origin of mourning has nothing to do with death,   it began on a battlefield that should have been won with kisses and hugs. There would be no one holding their children,   scared to know that all their stories about home are soluble in salt water.   This has nothing to do with betrayal,   or the lack of a love song for refugees,   or the debate of whether the solution for the cats left behind is to buy new cats   and name them after the seasons spent crossing the sea.   The origin of mourning began when the children grew taller than their father.   The origin of mourning began with theories   about why the moon does not feel hot, even when it shines brightest.

14

The origin of mourning began when the child in the restaurant closed her eyes.
The fire ate up her hair, and the fire extinguishers were faulty
or the waiters were too busy serving other customers.   I noticed the bird returned
straining to see how different she was from her last reflection.   The girl spilled the tea when
she opened her mouth to breathe.   I fear nothing about the night and the moon that was
the night's watch.   I fear the ground   for swallowing many bodies without spilling
their hearts. These tongues are pages of a diary that would be found many years away
settled down   in the stomach   of the river   that must be crossed.
Because I must leave home,   everyone expects I already know   how to swim.

NYCTOPHOBIA

Ghosts emerged
like shadows and mirages,
        and remained
        untouchable.

For now,
what stays buried
        may never stop
        growing

until your
reflection is
        blurred
        in the mirror.

What twirls
over your roof
        is either a kite
        or a missile

& what you seek
without looking
        will find its way
        through the dark.

PREACH

I

There is no perfect ending to any war.

There is no perfect ending
to what should not have had a beginning.

After the prayers,
the men yelled into the megaphones,

advertising aphrodisiacs, as they have
to men long dead or lost in the war.

II

A preacher asked that we prepare for eviction,
there's not enough time to save all we owned.

The death of the people we loved is
enough notice to us all.

This night sky hinted us about extinction,
but we were always busy—counting the stars.

Each time we shut our eyes, we moved closer
to an egress door—locked from the other side.

II

MOON

Kakuri

In the house where our ancestors lived,
I slept on a mat and faced the qibla.

The window was railed in small squares,
with cracks on the wall from where

the moon peeked through while we snored.
It could not be mistaken for an emergency exit.

I carried my brother on my shoulder,
he engraved our names

inside the squares on the ceiling.
We danced to the same song every night,

when the air was filled with the smell of burnt tires,
like it was on the eve of every new year.

The moon sifted its light through the cloud of smoke,
it was how God kept an eye on us, until fajr.

RAINBOW

Kosí ẹbi òṣùmàrè to parẹ́ nígbà tí ojo dá,
no one blames the light for this blindness.

Blame the ocean or its wave that wouldn't give up
any of the bodies it swallowed.

In prayers, beseech rainbow over this night sky,
like a mirror of olive oil on the skin that's fireproof.

Because there is salt in the blood,
on the beach, the boys hold hands in a circle

and tell stories they inherited
from their ancestors.

They hold their palms to the ears
like Baba, when he does the iqamaa.

Because it's rare he speaks in a foreign tongue
without stuttering.

With cupped hands, placed side by side,
he prayed to be outlived by all his boys.

There is no way to love them better,
instead, he calls them names he's afraid to call the sky.

FEATHERS

Inside a garden
haunted by echoes,

Baba taught me to make ink
from sugar.

I watched it turn brown
and then began to stir.

Fire conquered the granules
and melted them holy.

Because dead things can house a garden,
we carved pens from raffia.

On Baba's dusty shelves,
God's names were written in perfect rows.

We washed the slate into a keg,
a cup or two for our pregnant neighbors.

A nightingale arrived in a new country without a feather,
its calamus was carved into a weapon

sharp enough to write histories
of how we got our fingers stained in black.

PLANET

Say prayers in a foreign tongue,
God will not take offense

>   when we mutter the names
>   of our dead as a form of supplication.

In praise of the birds that perched by a window,
outside a universe of willows,

>   where the wind never carries any song
>   beyond the mouth of the mourners.

The lines beneath their feet
are the streams that dried out

>   in the silence of this planet.
>   We bury all we want growing

or we grow what should stay buried.
In a circle of spectators,

>   on a virgin field,
>   echoes are translated into qasida.

Earth is made of water and shadows,
forever, it will orbit round a pond of ghosts.

MYTH

We gathered in circles to unmake the myths of how the war shaped our tongues.
Another girl is moving out of this cycle into her new home.
Her friends gathered to dance around her, while she sang.

& in the gathered circles, we praised the sky—
too fast, I doubted it was in God's language.

I sat in a circle around a rectangular shaped piece of white fabric. Together
we chanted the names of Allah, until we got lost in the cluster of our own seeking.

At that moment, I believed the earth was the shape of a frying pan.
Everything that fit inside of it would lose it shape or maybe color,
but the pan always remained, no matter how hot it got.

Before we ate dinner, we listened to Baba tell stories
of the beginning, when we all were chewed lumps of flesh,
and before then, eggs waiting for the sun to ripen them into existence—

we were once forbidden—   nameless, or both.

THINGS I SAW IN MY FATHER'S EYES

were sparks of fireflies in a coal scuttle.
I did not ask him about the smuts on his eyelashes,
instead, I asked why the globe still reeked of smoke when world war
ended the year he was born.
You are too young to understand the almighty formula.
I asked when Mama would return from her
meeting with God in His house,
she had been away for years
& I was beginning to think the unspeakable.
You are too young to understand the almighty formula, he said
in a whisper that I grew up to know as the wind
that quenches the flame of a lantern, without
smashing the glass, sigh of grief that splotches
the shards of light, dying to see a new dawn.

ABECEDARIAN AS AN ATLAS FOR AWAKENING

Because my stomach is full of water, it means I thrive on what would kill me.
Cozenage of a dark room, full of pictures on transparent plastic films,
Designed on the sides with henna, they looked like postcards for men craving the sea.

Every child in this neighborhood learned to hold their breath underwater,
For that is how we can survive the memories of the floods.

Growing on the corners of our room are honeysuckles—their fragrances
Herald the memories that kept us up at night.

I pretended to be asleep when Baba made for the sea,
Jaborandi leaves tucked beneath the sides of his ears since they could not be
Knitted into a boat, to carry everyone whose names were etched on his rib bones.

Lying on the floor, I imagined he'd be back before sunrise.
My body became a pool, rippled with the belch of a frilled shark.

Next time I make it to the beach, I hope to grow gills
On this chest that has been a cupboard for a burnt atlas, kept together with
Purl stitches that now resemble the flag of a colony that no longer exists.

Quilts in different colors kept us from the cold and they
Remain evidence for our hastily packed bags for departure,
Since no one noticed that we headed for the sea without knowing how to swim.

To speak of the dead is to make a pot from what should have remained clay
Under this pink sky—a harbinger for awakened griefs, logged in stomachs, or
Vagary of prolonged drought, in a time when we needed the soil to break.

When the wind whistles, I sing along and drum the table that has the
Xylography of the past I don't want buried on the beach. I continue to

Yearn for a flicker on the face of the Mediterranean that will resemble
Zodiac signs for how we may survive, unlike the men before us.

KHALWA IN MY BABA'S GOWN

I held the warps of my sleeve's hem
between two fingers, and twisted them
into a rosary for khalwa.

Inside the incense burner, the bakhoor simmered
and filled the room with burnt fragrance
in silence—I scented grieving eyes.

Out of this cotton cave,
I untangled the rosary and weaved it
into a fish net, even though I was miles away from Sardis.

A night before I left Kaduna,
Baba reminded me of how my cry almost got them killed
months after my birth.

Each time he tells this story,
it ends in laughter, and a prayer
for Grandfather—buried inside a well.

The gown's overflowing sleeves were
gifts—for daring to swim across the sea
bearing scars of losing Grandfather to water.

I have a long history of resistance, so
I watered the aloe vera while in khalwa.
I have enough ointment to erase the scars on my body.

I opened my window and stared at the sky
with an ignited anger for all I have lost.

I know there's prayer in this silence ensued.
The pouch that houses a blade can't withstand its sharpness.

COSMOLOGY OF ON AN UNPAVED ROAD

Today I walked behind the woman for miles

and I mistook her shadow for an umbrella
or a satellite orbiting around a threaded ring.

Today the sky is a frozen mirror,
it refracts in exchange for more shadows.

Ghosts found shelter in a child's lungs
because the wind got thick.

Her reflection was in the water I drank,
but thirst rendered the eyes color-blind.

I followed her around an unpaved road
until she found an embassy for nightingales.

COLLAPSE

There is a flute in the air.
      It's a perforated matrix   of collagen fibers.

We danced when it was certain
      that the rain would be   heavy enough

to wash off the mud on our skin.

A million gallons of water escaped a dam,
      and the city was swept   into an exile of nothingness.

Boundaries were carved with the ruins, but
      the water continued   to run off the brown earth.

The sea became a pathway to escape the haunting echoes
      from rooms that were dented with hieroglyphs   or abbreviated prayers.

On the beach, a man promised to gift me a horse if I showed him my palms,
I chose to rather dance at the striking of its hooves on the wet sand.

Anytime I see a horse without a hostler,
      I whisper to myself: *This gift is a trap.*

I assume there is an army inside of it,
      waiting to attack.

That day, I imagined a papyrus basket would be found on the beach,
and a hawk would nest on the bones.

I imagined an ambulance would arrive,   with termites trapped in its headlights.

III

I can't tell you anything new about the river—
You can't tell a river to itself.

–Natalie Diaz

CURFEW

I

The war began on a school day.

I saw men walking around
with faces eclipsed by rage and grief.

The moon was fatigued
by its tawaf around earth.

II

I was born with hair on my shoulder,
Mama said I was kiniun in my previous life.

The scar on this forehead is a sign of reincarnation.
She told stories to distract us from the dying voices.

My Mama's eye was a theater for men
that praised the rusty edge of a blade

as they would a gate
that leads to a garden of proteas.

III

Wrinkles sprouted from the sides of her eyes
after the new millennium. Boys my age died in sleep.

On the sky that day were the stripes
of all ninety-nine shades of red.

We walked streets during the curfew
in search of florets,

and for the first time in weeks
I said a song in praise of my lunch box.

IV

We have all lost something, and in their memories,
we held a congregation in Kakuri market.

For once in our history that may go undocumented,
our scars flickered, as if caressed

by the yellow hands of a sleeping God.

EXODUS

I looked forward to the time / when I would join the queue /
outside a booth / coins in hand / waiting for my time /
to talk to someone on the phone / the war came
and we tucked our coins away / the telephone poles resisted the ebb /
but they became a sanctuary for pigeons / with nowhere else to go /
Mama told me all birds came from the deserts /
or they were the ghosts of pilgrims that didn't make it home from hajj /
the desert is the fastest route to the sea / and it has enough space
to bury the amulets that slow us down / we decided
we wanted to return with our thirst / and be baptized
in a salt pool / she stepped on a nail the day she was to leave /
it was an omen, but she's excited /
she is packed to meet with God in an arid land / like a wanderer
she left home with a bag / packed with pepper and antibiotics /
and a tongue that can only pray in Yoruba.

SUPPOSE IT RAINED IN HARMATTAN

Suppose everything beneath this sky
wasn't dying of loneliness—or hunger.

Suppose we sought a new God
that could not stand the sight of blood.

Suppose there's a new God in town,
and nothing edible goes on extinction.

Suppose we don't have to sing so high
for our prayers to be heard above machine noises.

Suppose we are not refugees in the land that holds our umbilical,
maybe Mama's hair will grow into a grain field

and each strand will flicker, like a wet nocturnal beetle,
as we gather to pray for rain in harmattan.

KHALWA WITH THE SONGBIRD OF WASSOULOU

I devoted this silence
to khalwa

or songs I heard about death
that began as love stories.

                    *

I sieved through the silence
for the songs Mama taught me

to keep my siblings quiet
in their bamboo cradles.

                    *

I saved my songs
for when it stopped raining.

Saa magni, dear blackbird,
tell me a story.

LANDSLIDE

Congo

I

Death is a genre of departure,
no one plans enough for it.

A second sandstorm unearths
tents buried in the first.

This town is full of survivors
and victims of the wind.

II

A new city emerged
from the red earth.

Its newness weathered
when the sun set.

III

In a town that holds
filaments of dead lights

there was a landslide, sadly—
it buried everyone caught sleeping.

BATS

I

What song would you render
on the eve of another storm?

In this prayer house, bats perched
on the speaker beside the pulpit.

I believed they could hear us,
and like the old days

we spoke in tongues
to reconnect with our ancestors,

but I don't know what God made of it.

II

This was the earliest miracle
I knew: they were without food for three days

and they left at almost the same time—
after maghrib prayer.

I still don't know what bats eat.

III

I was relieved when the bats flew out the window,
back into the night sky, where every miracle belongs.

SELF PORTRAIT AS A BEACH

I do not mean anything that comes out
of my mouth tonight,
being drunk and hungry have similar symptoms.
I feel stupid saying this
without any scientific proof.
You would be the first I would tell this,
I have no problem with my tongue, although
I say things slightly different from what I mean.
I am a beach & always wet,
I know you think of something else.
I have been a beach all my life.
The wound across my face is purpled
like a premature rainbow over the sky
that washes down after a drizzle.
But like the beach that I am, memories
hide beneath the swollen skin.
What is left with me are broken eyeglasses,
missing pairs of children's shoes, and
misplaced wedding rings—that are better left misplaced.

SEISMICITY

Agadir, Morocco

A radio with no antenna hung on the mud fence.
Cocooned with moths flying around it, their brown wings resembled
a lake after rainfall, with oil spreading through its center to the edges.
This was the year of Independence in Nigeria, but eight months before the sky
gleamed to the dancing congregation on the beach in Lagos. Baba was seated outside
a mosque with tesbihi in his right hand, he continued to chant prayers beneath his breath.
That night, Agadir would split open. The cracked façade would be hidden in the darkness.
More than half the town was swallowed in the same ground they placed their foreheads to in prayers.
Everything lost in the night was excavated and buried again after mass janazah.
A new country germinated from the dead one. Now, on the balcony of a hotel
as you watch the sunrise above the sea, do you recognize the scar on its face?
All you see is an illumination of a giant god that keeps taking a rest when the sky is soaked.
The healed wounds are now erased in the salt water, after it kept rowing them back to the beach.
When they thought the apocalypse was here they found their way
to continue to sing, because a new country was liberated. They sat on the balcony to drink tea
and say prayers for what they lost that was not found in the rubble, they told stories
to the children, of how long a night is if you search for a lover in a grave you did not dig.

43

DEW

I found a key
to the old house on a beach.

Trapped in a wooden box,
love letters and a ring.

Memory fades with each passing day.
Dew collected

on the apex of a leaf,
trickled into the puddle

on the ground.

At full moon,
my eyes were bleached in the light.

I lifted my curtain
after days of khalwa,

Broken neck
of a guitar in my hands,

I marveled at the blame
of what happened to its shriveled strings,

without knowing how
to finger a song from what was now broken.

Aftermath of a tsunami,
the palm trees were washed away

with all the birds that nested in them.

SUDAN

for the last male white rhino

Today is a new year in Antarctica,
so I found a rib bone on a bookshelf.

The death of Sudan surrounds us with a queer reflux.
I know this survival depends on how long

the body can keep everything green
until it no longer resembles what grows on any tree.

There is no one to tell about the fallen stars,
and the clouds that veiled how bright

his eyes shone in the absence of the sun.
It snows outside, and I wish we could

make it across the Nile this night
because this vacuum needs a song.

I wonder if it's a sign of a second coming,
or if the wound on his body was the map of Nile

before it shrank within her skeleton.
For now, his eye is the size of everything it sees.

COSMOLOGY OF EXTINCTIONS

I

Every ocean that has tried to kill me
was made stronger,

except when a ship broke down
in the middle of it,

leaking black oil
into a coral reef.

The oil film concealed the sunlight
from the photic zone,

until savaged. A blood moon
sat over the ocean.

How do I rescue
what is rendered homeless

without crossing the border?

II

On this day, two centuries ago,
a child rescued a quagga from drowning,

feathers of a dodo
clenched between his teeth.

III

On that same day,
snores of whales were blurred

by flapping rotor blades, and
the sputter was a prayer

to the ears of a dying orangutan.

IV

Dandelions sprouted
on the graves of elephants

buried without their tusks.

Their shadows are clustered
inside an amphitheater.

With every death
a flute is emptied of its music.

RAIN-MAKER

There was a girl dancing in the rain,
   her gown grew bigger with each twirl.
She was happy to have learned to fly without asking anyone
   about birds and the origin of spacecraft.
The rain stopped when the first spade hit the soil.
   Another was buried before sunset.
Will this earth ever find a voice for "satisfaction"?
   Each death was a step towards extinction.
Toys are arranged around the sides of a tub
   although no one is coming for a bath.
Compost is all that will become of the memories
   hidden in the marrow, along with the cadmium and iron
that have become too heavy to be purged through her sweat.
   This is about the girl in the rain and her soft-red gown.
Extinction is when it rains and there is no girl to dance in it,
   or the girl fears that the cloud may turn from blue litmus to red.
This girl has lived in different cities, although in her previous life
   she had no name on her forehead,
or it was wiped away by the fire, or the gas, or the bullets
   before the water that surrounds the world
shrank,
   before the ocean was halved by the bulk of plastics.
I go fishing in Nile because it reminds me of my childhood,
   and of the women that had worn its waves around their waists.
Nile is my grandmother curled up in a cradle,
   I do not know what song to sing to remind her
of how I was born with the weight of a baby elephant.
   All along, I thought it was my dance that made it rain.

MERCURY

In this grassland,
every room

is a sacred chamber
for grieving

or a cubicle for khalwa.

Overnight,

a whale returned
to the sea, wounded—

calabash was
carved out of its meat.

The beach remains
bald of evidence.

Like my body, it's a planet
coated with sour memories.

I fear it will be invaded
by strangers who'll promise

to rescue me
from the ruins I was born in.

CURE

I am a picnic away from a breakup
or sleep, away from dementia.

On the brownfield, white willows thrived
from the bodies that germinated beneath.

Spiders made a ward of what remained
in the broken kitchen after the war.

We had calendars to track our disasters,
since the lines on our palms translate

to the Arabic numerals for eighteen
and eighty-one. I was taught

about nomenclatures of vacant eyes,
or departures that began after the echoes.

Once, I believed the creases on our palms
remind us of the ninety-nine names of Allah,

until I discovered God had a name
in every tongue I could not speak—

some palmar creases do not touch,
and some skins are shed in harmattan.

As a cure for what we survived
that has refused to kill us in our sleep,

I watch the sunrise and wonder
if it's ever gotten tired of the routine.

STORM

I

The rainstorm quenches all that burns
with no less destruction than the fire.

Here, graveyards are demarcated
with sugarcanes, as if

to sweeten the buried memories—
until Israfil trumpets.

I fear the whistling in the wind
anytime we drive by,

I fear being recognized
by the dead I once escorted.

II

I held a child in my hands
because he was too small for a bier.

He was killed by what I survived.
After a naming ceremony,

I stood behind Baba as he led the prayer—
we chorused *Amen*,

but I know the storm will be back
before the next full moon.

BEACH

Mississippi, 2020

Because the water smells,
I say a qasida to the God of dead things.

On the lake in Sardis,
a squadron of white pelicans

swims back and forth
to hinder the water from freezing.

On this side of the beach,
littered with feathers and fishbones,

"Do Not Swim / No Lifeguard"
is printed in bold letters.

I am not lonely enough
to desire a swim in winter—

if I did, I wouldn't get to listen
to the song from a young shepherd

on the other side of the beach.
He fingers a tenor guitar

and sings into a clapping wave.

ACKNOWLEDGMENTS

Poems from this collection have appeared in the following publications:

The Kenyon Review: "Blue"

Scoundrel Times: "Exodus" & "Suppose it Rained in Harmattan"

Four Way Review: "Abecedarian as an Atlas for Awakening" & "Cosmology of Baba as the Rainmaker"

Coffee House Poetry: "Curfew"

Poetry Magazine: "Bats"

Malahat Review: "Prayer," "Khalwa With the Songbird of Wassoulou," & "Cure"

Prairie Schooner: "Things I Saw in My Father's Eyes"

EcoTheo Review: "Rainmaker" & "Sudan"

Up the Staircase Quarterly: "Origin of Mourning"

Sugar House Review: "Feathers"

Glass Poetry Journal: "Self Portrait as a Beach"

The Journal: "Wi-Fi in a Floating Colony"

Poetry Northwest: "Rainbow"

Poet Lore: "Moon"

Willow Springs: "Myth" & "Planet"

This book exists because of the support and generosity of the University of Mississippi's MFA program. Thanks to my teachers, Melissa Ginsburg, Derrick Harriell, Ann Fisher-Wirth, Adetayo Alabi, Beth Ann Fennelly, and everyone in the English Department.

A special thank you to my teacher and mentor Aimee Nezhukumatathil for her resourcefulness and insightful comments that helped shape this book. Thank you for your kindness, for the many plates of food, and to Dustin Parson for bringing me torchlight and chocolates when it was dark.

Thank you to friends and colleagues who at one point read and provided feedback for some of the poems. Thank you Andy Sia, Nadia Alexis, Joshua Nguyen, Noel Quinones, Ellie Black, O-Jeremiah Agbaakin, Lenna Mendoza, Marina Leigh, Christy Conner, Mike Pontacoloni, Gabriel Mundo, Kate Leland, Mason Wray, Linda Flynn, Michael Martella, Joanna, Ida Harris, Stacy Balkun, Rae Delbianco, Marina Greenfeld, Siyun Fang, Maggie Graber, Christopher Morris.

Thank you Sadia Hassan for holding my hands through the storm and to friends who listened to my stories.

ABOUT THE AUTHOR

Hussain Ahmed is Nigerian, poet, and environmentalist. He holds an MFA from the University of Mississippi and is currently a PhD student at the University of Cincinnati. His poems have appeared in *American Poetry Review*, *Poetry Magazine*, *The Kenyon Review*, *A Public Space*, and elsewhere. He is the author of the chapbook *Harp in a Fireplace* (Newfound, 2021) and the poetry collection *Soliloquy With the Ghosts in Nile* (Black Ocean Press, 2022).

ABOUT ORISON BOOKS

Orison Books is a 501(c)3 non-profit literary press focused on the life of the spirit from a broad and inclusive range of perspectives. We publish books of exceptional poetry, fiction, and non-fiction from perspectives spanning the spectrum of spiritual and religious thought, ethnicity, gender identity, and sexual orientation.

As a non-profit literary press, Orison Books depends on the support of donors. To find out more about our mission and our books, or to make a donation, please visit www.orisonbooks.com.

Orison Books is deeply grateful to our recurring annual donors for sustaining our important work. If you'd like to make a recurring or one-time contribution, please visit www.orisonbooks.com/support-us.

Sustainers' Circle

Carol Dines
Michele Laub
Laura & Barry Rand
Bruce Spang
Lee Stockdale
Anonymous

Advocates' Circle

David Ebenbach
Anonymous

Supporters' Circle

Nickole Brown
Richard Chess

Friends' Circle

Paige Gilchrist
Laurel Haavik
Alida Woods